# of a man

MATT SMYTHE

REVISION OF A MAN

Matt Smythe

DEAD RECKONING
20
17
COLLECTIVE

Copyright © 2022 Matt Smythe

All rights reserved.
This book or any portion thereof
May not be used or reproduced in any fashion whatsoever
Without the permission of the publisher or the author
Except for the use of quotations

Publisher: Dead Reckoning Collective
Book Cover Design: Tyler James Carroll
Book Cover Photo: Matt Smythe

Printed in the United States of America

ISBN-13: 978-1-7376686-8-8 (paperback)

PRAISE FOR *REVISION OF A MAN*

“Poet Louis Simpson, a straight-talking WWII Battle of the Bulge veteran, once said that the difference between strong and weak poetry is that when reading the real thing, we have the constant feeling that it *had* to be written. Simpson had suffered, had problems after the war. This was not something to speak lightly about. He wanted a poetry that didn't fuck around, that had us by the ears and throats. I think I could speak safely for him to say that Matt Smythe's *Revision of a Man* would have held and shaken him.

This is a book of unrelenting honesty, yes, but also of poetic voltage, poem after poem, relation after relation. Smythe tells us—as he ranges his life as soldier/husband/ father/hunter/angler and more—that "I'm trying to find my own context" as he tries, despite his devils and wildnesses, his "destructive blind runs," to get his voice, as he says, home. Well, this powerful book is that home he has found and made. It never evades as he witnesses himself and our condition.”

William Heyen, National Book Award Finalist
Author of *The Candle: Poems of Our Twentieth Century Holocausts*

"Like water rings in reverse, Matt Smythe’s poems gather inward toward a center of deep, profound sentiment, whether they are examining the rigors of military life, the sudden flush of a brook trout or the many blooms of fatherhood. Pervading each carefully chosen word, each memorable line, is a force of feeling that will be instantly recognizable to those who have lived hard and loved true. These poems don’t just tell a story. They tell a life.”

Dave Karczynski
Lecturer, University of Michigan, Ann Arbor

“Matt Smythe writes his world with the relentless, thousand-yard stare of a soldier and the wide-eyed detail and Zen wonderment of an outdoorsman. It’s an unlikely mix, and his work can be jolting and brutal one moment, poignant and lovely the next. Whether describing a bloody bar fight or his most candid internal moments, Smythe hides nothing and searches for everything in this remarkable, unflinching collection.”

Steve Duda
Managing Editor for Fly Fishing, Patagonia

"In *Revision of a Man*, Matt Smythe writes expansive lyric poems with a keen and haunting clarity: poems of struggle, poems of pleasure, poems caught up in the matrix of war, poems voiced with stunning tenderness.

Smythe's poetry shapes and makes whole the material of experience, gives form to fleeting moments, and makes permanent the ephemeral: "In an instant the tangle flexes,/untangles/and is gone."

This book is a moving and powerful portrait of a man re-seeing the world, not in innocence, but through the complexity of experience."

Eric Pankey, Professor of English
Heritage Chair in Writing at George Mason University

"Matt Smythe is in a league of his own when it comes to making every word matter. He is among the best 'outdoor poets' of this generation."

Kirk Deeter
Editor-in-Chief, Trout Unlimited Media

"Some poets write about a rarified idea of life, that parallel world where an awakened self has occasion to listen and share oracular truths wistfully wrapped in gauzy revelation.

Matt Smythe's poems do not look to that world but instead speak vulnerably from within the one we inhabit in our usual state of uncertainty and longing.

Whether through the voice of a young soldier navigating the threshold between boredom and duty, a new father daring to promise his child a future free of paternal grief, or an outdoorsman enveloped in the inexplicable language of nature, Matt Smythe's poems speak from within our actual world — the place that either batters us into wisdom or blessedly abandons us to wondrous befuddlement."

Jon Palzer, Professor of Creative Writing & Literature
Finger Lakes Community College

ACKNOWLEDGEMENTS

Deal first appeared in
Southern Culture on the Fly

The fine line between flight and inertia first appeared in
The Mission

The sound of one soldier dying first appeared in
Blueline

West to water and *The gory details* first appeared in
The Fly Fish Journal

Shooting darts in Alaska first appeared in
Revive Fly Fishing Journal

Over Montana. His first mountains., Naknek August, Origin's Name, Prodigal Sockeye and When you hold an Alaskan Salmon first appeared in
TROUT Magazine

This current's course first appeared in
Gray's Sporting Journal

The consequence of rain first appeared in
The Finger

A front pushes in first appeared in
The Drake

"If my devils are to leave me, I'm afraid my angels will take flight as well."

-Rainer Maria Rilke

To the ones who always saw me, even when I wasn't.
Thank you.

PREFACE

DEAL

When I was 4 or 5,
I watched my mother carrying me into the hospital.
From above, like the blackbirds floating against blue,
heads cocked, I watched. Fading into and out of the dark.
The sun is barely over Bare Hill. Certain thoughts should not be
given this much light. Summer is over at the speed I'm driving.
This road heads south.

At the end of this backbone will be the promised land, I'm sure.
Signs in truck stop windows tell me on the way in,
cleanest restrooms.
On the way out, please come again!
I can't say I won't. I've been here before.

Oh to reach that promised land. Oh to drive until daylight's gone.
Oh to drive all night.
Oh to find cheap gas.
Oh why the hell am I leaving?
Oh road (you'd better be worth it).

12:38 am somewhere between Beckley and the Appalachians.
The waitress smokes between tables.
Seven truckers use payphones.
Two elderly couples are having eggs, toast and sausage.
My coffee is half gone. The waitress slides over with a refill, winks.
She never brought the bill.
I left $2 and an empty mug.

Dreams come. Almost always they involve great heights.
Rooftops, cliffs, mountain tops, bridges.
I'm always surrounded by people I know but do not recognize.
There's always a woman. Always a woman there.
I wake as she allows me to touch her. It is never daylight. This time
I'm parked at an abandoned gas station.

Columbus, Georgia.
The old bar hasn't changed except for the employees.
It's been 10 years. A beer for old-time's sake.
A second for the emptiness.
It's an off night. Stale and overwhelmingly quiet.
I wanted the place to be packed like it was when I left.

Once I saw a gator snatch a deer by the head
and drag it flailing into a small lake near here.
We were fishing for bass in a 15-foot john-boat
along a weed bed 50 yards from the explosion.
The deer was quietly sipping at the shore.
We left the water ringing with
the growing concentric silence and
blackbirds lighting out from the trees.
Years later blackbirds still remind me.

I don't drive through Fort Benning to my old barracks.
I don't stop for cheap gas
or to buy an air assault sticker from US Cavalry.
I do make a couple phone calls to answering machines.
I forgot everything just across the bridge in Phenix City (Alabama).

I was used to forgetting in these parts.
I had been this way with Eric (road trip, Memphis).
Graceland would set us free and his Honda Civic would get us there.
He hadn't changed the oil in almost 10,000 miles.
It was dead Elvis week. We forgot about the Army.
We drank all the way. We mocked the King.
We stumbled down Beale Street.

Beale street at night. It hadn't moved, but something in me did.
Everything did.
I sat down on the curb. I was 100 years old right then.
Left over and full of nothing.
That night I made a deal with myself over the toilet.
I had made this deal before with whiskey and beer.
There's something empowering about making a deal.
The finality is settling.

When sleep came, it was like I was dead.
Blackbird-black and real quiet.
I'd like to believe that. When you die nothing comes and gets you.
Nothing snatches you away screaming to the fire and pain.
When I die,
I'll just slip back into the dark like a bass returned to its shadows.

BLOOD & SERVICE

OF BLOOD I'VE BEEN TOLD

The breeze lies on the water.
There are two red canoes with four people in
blue lifejackets paddling with silver and black paddles.
The maples have pushed out their leaves to hang limp,
yellow-green and newborn.
The reflection of boats docked to the shore waver
in the wake of one goose moving toward the island.
At one time that goose had been in flight on a southern course.
At one time it had been feeding in New York corn stubble.

———

A deer lowers its head to fallen acorns,
walks into the breeze proud and knowing.
Empty mouths cry in the valley.
Sun falls patched on leaf, moss and maple sprout alike, burning the
frosted collar from our shoulders.
Wind lies still in the valley.
The sun goes cold over the hills. It will warm to greet us again soon.
Our young will grow with the seasons. Nothing is lost.
Buckskin blankets in the valley. Our mouths full of song.

———

From Indian Falls, Algonquin's jagged head is
framed by pine, rock, water and sky.
Snow is alive on valley currents.
Lifting my eyes from winking coals and hiss of unseasoned branches,
through the smoke
I create the peak, frame its jagged head, hear the wind
through the pine boughs.
Snowflakes land white and new on my jacket, pause, then glisten.

———

Lithe long fingers—
Her gray smolders burgundy, then faint green.
Japanese maple moving, then still—
Her graceful, tangled sweep of stars
bows to the breeze and rippled water.

———

I am up early enough this morning to watch the carpenter bee that nests in the rafter above the doorway where I sit begin her day.
Her buzz interrupted my train of thought about three deer I had seen in the field below our house drinking from the stream.
Humming above and behind me, I tip my head back to watch her hover just below the beam of the doorway.
Her wings, dark auras that hold fast to her back and forth motion—
I can feel their wash on my face.
Her day of hunting for pollen grains or soft wood to masticate has begun.
Legs folded dutifully to abdomen, she re-examines the territory around her nest, finds me incidental and moves on.

———

Canoe in dark water.
Silent bow with no wake, no foam, no waves crashing.
Turtles sun quietly on their flotilla of logs.
Herons slow-step along green shores with careful eyes for minnows.
Bushes full of white sound below yellow pine.
Bass breathe thick shadows under lilies.

———

I was smaller than my sister when my dad told the story of the stones, Indian heads, hard heads, smooth-solid and half buried in shale flakes below the high banks at the south end of the lake.
Seneca, Canandaigua.
These waters are the print of the Great Spirit's hand, the story goes.
Cayuga, Owasco.
These hills grew from between the Spirit's fingers and the valleys beyond them.
Skaneateles, Keuka, Otisco.
My people were born of this place, of many places. Skulls turned to stone in death.
Smaller ones were those of children my size.
Honeoye, Hemlock
I picked them out of ankle-deep water, asking—*this one? And this?*
Deeper the lake at my belly, I would find larger stones with bare feet and stand on their easy angles like pale green hillsides.

———

I stand on this hill, above other hills, above valleys.
I stand before this land shouldered teeming wildlife.
I stand before the nations I was told the French soldiers attacked
while the men were away hunting.
I was told, if I remain after nightfall, spirits that still defend this place
will turn the breath in my chest to ash.
For now, while sundown rests on these hills,
they whisper to me from the grass.
I close my eyes, listen across the distance.
It is enough that I hear their voices,
share their steps under this sky of fire.

IMPRINT

Sucker Brook was only fish part of the time.
It was always crayfish and shale and a copper-colored bed.

It was hellgrammites. It was tiny leeches
between puckered toes after wading an entire afternoon.

It was never dipping a line in that water even once—
instinct never registering in my boyhood
mind to do anything else but wade in it, play in it,
scrape my knees on its rocks.

In me was a greedy curiosity for water, for the outdoors,
for the uncharted backwoods bird, animal, fish-filled places
where I felt hidden.

But water spoke the loudest—
wooed me before dawn, straight through lunch and dinner
and on into firefly evenings.

CEMETERY SPRING RUN

When my dad was a boy, Sucker Brook would run black in the spring with redhorse suckers. From a steady farm field spring through Woodlawn Cemetery, the brook filled pools and bends, cut under banks leaving tree roots exposed, slowed under each of the four cemetery bridges and then made its way under Pearl street through the elementary school grounds, passing under Gibson St., West Ave., Chapin St., Bristol St., Clark St. and Parrish St. where it widened, yawned under routes 5 and 20, passed the public boat launch and sluggishly joined the north end of Canandaigua Lake just west of the city pier. The fish would travel this course in reverse to pack into the cemetery in spawn.

Woodlawn Cemetery was 77 acres and 70 percent wooded. When my dad was a boy he would wade at night, a Coleman lantern in one hand illuminating a ten-foot circle of thrashing fish, and a three-pronged spear and the other. Fish so thick they bumped his legs as if they were simply branches or rocks like all the other branches or rocks they bumped to that point. You had to have very good awareness of where your feet were within that cloud of rioting fish.

When I started wading around in the cemetery, dad showed me how to lay on my belly and feel along under the banks, gently moving my hand over roots and stones, slowly so as to not spook any fish. Having seen a few of these giant big-bodied fish holding lazily to the bottom in a downstream pool, sticking my hand under the bank to grab one made me nervous.

A fish belly felt exactly as I expected a fish belly to feel. Cold. Smooth. Living. Feeling past pectoral fins up to the base of the gills, making a C shape with my fingers and thumb, a yelp and a lunge and snatch and I lifted the monster from its cave—water dripping from my face and chest and belly an arm. Water dripping from the fish. Fish flexing with the strength of every fish I'd ever held. Ever seen. Ever would see. Child muscles taught and tan. My dad whooping on the far bank.

THREE WAYS OF LOOKING AT MY FATHER

Let me tell you a story:
After hunting and in the old Ford pick-up he bought in just good enough shape for carrying wood he'd split after felling a dead tree or dragging one out of a tangle of ivy and underbrush in Woodlawn Cemetery, my dad hit a deer while driving home one evening.

On a road where pavement was still years away and the fields that shouldered up to it hadn't yet began to aspirate the words salt or traffic, the buck bounded into the path of dad's truck, crushed the bumper, grill and hood and landed on the gravel as dad came to a skidding halt. The buck stood, shook its head and finished its run for the woods.

Another:
Years before I knew that my fists could draw blood, dad told me that if I ever had to fight that I should fight like my life depended on it—fight like the other guy had my death in mind.

This after a story about having to defend a friend outside a bar called the Purple Pig. His friend was fall-down drunk and two strangers with a tire-iron and brick meant to take advantage of the situation. Dad took the tire-iron and the consciousness of one and part of the other's nose—spat it like tobacco in the dust of the parking lot.

Another:
I had nightmares when I was a kid—waking for no reason other than premonition, I'd open my eyes, look at the end of the bed and catch the shadow of my grandmother just before she ducked from view.
I'd whisper for her to come out—
I saw you, I'd say.
It's not funny anymore.

In the soundlessness of a sleeping house I'd raise my voice and yell at nothing crouched beyond the foot of my bed until dad would come in with the light and make me look for myself.

What of resilience?
What of the blood of loyalty?
What of the things we need to let go?

Backing into a driveway, a woman who is not paying attention drives the speed limit into my door. Unconscious for twenty minutes, I wake while being pulled from the back of an ambulance knowing who I am and that someone needs to call my dad, but I can't remember his number and I ask about the paint job on my truck.

After four beers and a twenty-minute drive, five of us get out of my truck in front of a Nuremberg club within eyeshot of The Wall and its siren red light. Another soldier tries to sucker my friend with a beer bottle, but I intervene, threatening to break his neck—hand at his throat, my knuckles bloody. He apologizes. Buys me a beer.

Before dawn on the 31st of July, 1990, carrying a duffle packed with less than what I used to take to summer camp, I climb into a van with government plates with six other sons bound for Syracuse, then Missouri, to learn how to be Combat Engineers and defend our country. Out the back window I see dad say goodbye in sign language —*I love you.*

SEPTEMBER, 1990

My first and only Missouri fall
smells of fresh-turned earth,
a must-heavy canvas tent
and my military issued t-shirt
drying after a hard day's work.

Sunset has retreated completely now.
Dark shadows turn into enemy troops,
then back to logs, bushes and trees.
My eyes are unreliable,
I listen.

Miles away and A-10 flies night
maneuvers 150 feet above tree-line.
Gatling guns roar downrange.

It's that far away and still that loud.

It's the night,
darkness makes everything feel closer.

It's been days since I thought about home.
I stop listening and try to bring back their faces.
Not *everything* feels closer in darkness.

In five days I'll be able to see them again—
to open my wall-locker and look
at their pictures taped to the inside of the door.

Five more nights I'll lie in this foxhole,
identify shadows,
listen to the distant beat in my chest.

SELF PORTRAIT, 1991.
A SOLDIER IN GERMANY

My seasons were different.
Weather back home was a fleeting interest
as I pointed just below Lake Ontario on the TV—
a weatherman motioning open-handed
to the low-pressure system heading south over the Finger Lakes.
I lit a cigarette,
blew a cloud at the screen.

ONE YEAR

I have been in country a year. I speak enough German to get a cold beer, identify road signs, ask *wo ist der bahnhof* and hit on girls (even though they all speak English) and the Beastie Boys opened for Public Enemy on my 20th birthday. When we cruise in my truck, which is dropped, tinted and packed with speakers, we shake windows and brain cells with our music but more importantly we turn heads. Female heads to be specific. I had a Buck knife that I had found somewhere two weeks ago, slashed a complete set of tires on a car that belongs to a guy who pissed me off last night at a bar and then threw it in some random front yard of some random house on some random street that we sped down. There is a barbecue most every weekend that the weather is nice. Music, food, malt liquor, women, basketball. An African guy slapped a girl we know in a club we hang out in, so we chased him out. He and his friends threw bottles out of a fourth-floor window at us, so we counted windows up and over and headed for the stairs. One got hit with a bat and got away, the other got shot right in front of me and we ran. I've had five different roommates after *quality of life* began. The first pissed his bed after drinking too much. He was out quick. The second had a serious girlfriend who told me that she wasn't as serious as he was, and I tried to tell him, but he called me a liar and found a new room. Two others finished their time in the unit and went stateside. The last one I became good friends with, but I wound up moving into my own room with no roommate. I run the streets every night except Mondays (because there is nothing to do on Monday) and usually make it home with just enough time to get dressed for PT and go. I am an American blue-eyed-blonde-haired novelty and I take advantage of every pretty face with big tits every chance I get. Fest beer costs 8 marks and the mug always goes home with me. A steady paycheck and no bills lets me do whatever the hell I want. Some guy wanted to fight because he said I was looking at him, so we took it outside and he acted tough in front of the crowd that gathered, but I could tell he had never really been in a fight before. I'm not sure where I learned how to fight, but I told him *I'll kill you before I hurt you*, followed immediately with a punch that broke his nose and blind rage till I'm pulled off him. There's been a few scuffles like that. At work I drive a forklift, moving ammunition from bunkers to flatbed trailers that are bound for Saudi or the US. We work 20-hour days all the time. I sleep while I drive, don't ask me how I do it. We buy cartons of smokes and bottles of rum on our ration cards for next to nothing. I know a guy who has lifted over 600 CD's from the PX over the course of a month. He always has hash too. There is always something desperate in how we act. Like if we don't get drunk, don't get laid, don't steal something, don't fight, don't have loud music, don't do something —anything—there will be no tomorrow. My life is habit.

SELF PORTRAIT, 1993.
A SOLDIER IN GERMANY

I am close to where the camera-man captured Hitler
in black and white for his propaganda films.

I recognize the stone bleachers
despite passing decades,
bullet pocks and lack of pomp.
The weight of the past sits squarely on this place.
I can hardly breathe.

I have been here their whole life—a soldier
among the youth of this country—
but I don't see the blood on their hands.
See the smoke from the camps.
Put my hands on the cold, wood slats of the box cars. I don't
turn around and stare into the young
face of the gate guard at Dachau
while 5-ton trucks roared past heaped piles
of soil and lime barely covering the recent dead.

I'm trying to find my own context.
I'm trying to picture this sleepy city—
with its food vendors and sex shows
and young faces and night clubs playing American music—
with tanks rumbling through the streets.
Buildings as shadows,
skeletons in the heavy mist.
Snipers in church towers
and everything in black and white—
soldiers,
panzers,
barbed-wire,
cobblestone streets,
the recent dead.

I am not this thoughtful.
This is not me.

THE RIVER DID NOT WEEP

Imagine the Chattahoochee River.
Meandering minor Mississippi with the same amount of mud.
The stretch that borders Ft. Benning in Georgia is bound
by black willow, cypress, cottonwood, pawpaw, kudzu, beaver, heron,
cottonmouth, chiggers and cicada heat.

I was there when the Rangers loaded
the C-130 for night-jump training.
I was there when the plane took off and flew
a five-mile circle before approaching the drop zone nap-of-the-earth.
I was there when they stood up, hooked up to the static line
and waited on the green light.
I was there when the last seven were rushed by their First Sergeant
out the door and into the night after the jump window had passed.

The First Sergeant followed on the heels of the last Ranger.
The last seven dropped silently except for
the soft whip-billow of their parachutes,
into the tangle of undergrowth at the treeline,
into the riverside trees,
into the night-black Chattahoochee.

All but the First Sergeant were found alive
and when taps was played for the fallen Ranger
the river did not weep.

FALL IN

Lightning struck a platoon of basic trainees standing in formation in the parking lot of a rifle range, just as the cattle trucks pulled in to transport them back to their barracks.

There were about twenty boys that caught the bolt.
They were pale, shaking, mumbling, crying, staring blankly at me.

Like a bomb went off in the middle of us.

They just fucking flew.

I'm so cold.

I couldn't hear my voice when I spoke—

Look right here at me.
You're going to be all right.
What's your name?
Stay with me now.

WHEN I WAS JODY.
WHEN I WAS A SOLDIER.

I knew guys that went AWOL and committed suicide over Jody. Jody was a pimp fighting a war. We used to make up verses about Jody when we marched to help us with our cadence
Buddy Stewart, singer/band leader

He sho nuff could satisfy
Jean Knight, New Orleans soul artist

Ain't no use in goin home,
Jody's got your girl and gone.

Sing of me soldiers of fortune,
comrades in arms, friends of mine.
I stand in your ranks, much closer
than you think.

Better hope you keep your head,
Jody's got your girl in bed.

You'd kill to have a shot
with that rifle of yours
(I know I'd use mine)
while I'm eating your dessert.

Ain't no use in lookin down,
Jody's headin for your town.

I ran in your packs,
drinking beer and whiskey,
sniffing after late night
romps in foreign beds.

Ain't no use in bein mad,
face it soldier, you been had.

Sing, I say, sing about that fuck
in all of us. Sing it loud,
left, right, left, right, left—
sing it till you believe it.

Ain't a damn thing you can do,
the Army'll make you a Jody too.

THE SOUND OF ONE SOLDIER DYING

When you go, he said,
they all said,
again and again,
when you go most of you are going to die.
What in god's name was I supposed to do with that knowledge?

What power to be handed death—
to be given the future.

I believed him.
Them.
I believed them again and again.

**

A Ranger had pictures and the lower half of his body still bandaged from a grenade as souvenirs from Rwanda.
They would fly helicopters right outside the jump door, he said, *machine guns just screaming, guys dead before the static line popped their chute.*
He smiled when I asked about the Geneva Convention—*yea, right.*
He tipped a black-and-white photo of a C-130 in a hard bank with a sheet of flares deployed in the other direction—the surface-to-air missile in the bottom left corner.
This was from our bird, I had a disposable hidden.
This shit never makes the paper either.

**

When a man is shot in another country and he is alone, does anyone hear the air leave his lungs?
When a town in another country is bombed and bombed and bombed and bombed does anyone hear the planes before they are shadows on the streets?

**

A mural painted on the end of a barracks in Ft. Leonard Wood, Missouri:
Sweat more in peace, bleed less in war.

**

He has three boys and a daughter on the way and he can't play with them. Something in the grit and powder of that Saudi sand, permeating his food, his boots, his rifle, his ruck, his uniform, his eyes, his nostrils, his lungs, knotting his body and mind, making his nightmares indistinguishable from the everyday.

He is older than his father, older than his grandfather.
His wife is tired, used to be the girl all the boys lusted after in high school.
His disease is her burden.
Her burden is pulling her apart.
They have three boys and a daughter on the way.
The boys look just like their dad.

**

Twenty-five years old and already awarded the Purple Heart.
He's recovered completely from the five gunshots and escaping Somalia, he says.
I'm staying in, he says.
He doesn't say much else. Drinks beer, stays quiet.
I work at the bar with his fiancée.
He proposed when he got out of the hospital.
She brings him another bottle when he finishes—
won't talk about his staying in.
Between tables she sits next to him looking tiredly at her hands.
The battery in her watch died weeks ago, but she checks it out of habit.
Time has stopped and he's still alive.

**

When his time came, we were in the mess hall.
No one knew he was that far gone.

The buffer—
industrial duty, made for polishing long military hallways
to a high-gloss—
hung by its industrial-duty cord just two feet from the ground.
A broken soldier at the other end.

Returning from the mess hall we saw
the buffer bump and sway gently against the brick.

We thought it strange that our best buffer found its way out of a third-story window. Someone was going to catch hell for it.

**

The Army is only required to give soldiers four hours of sleep
in a twenty-four-hour period.
In order to move the requisite amount of munitions to and from Saudi through our ammo supply point we became very familiar with this regulation.
Sleep rarely came during my four hours off.
Sleep came while driving
a 4,000-pound variable reach Skytrak forklift.
Sleep came while I was stacking
multi-launch-rocket-systems on flat bed trailers.

Sleep came when I was wheeling
full pallets of fragmentation grenades out of bunkers.
Sleep came while I was nudging
rows of artillery rounds just a few inches further onto a truck.
$144 million-worth of military-grade middle fingers
raised proudly in my sleep.

**

We have become the strongest driven by our collective pride
and our young, ambitious history.
We have stood against tyranny, freed ourselves from it.
We have existed forever in expatriate passion
and the lifting of the self through knowledge.
We are the land of the free.
We are the land of milk and honey.
We will be a home to your huddled masses.
We have a conscience.

We have become the strongest out of pride in spite of our history
of no man created equal.
We have stood as tyrant, enslaved in the name of progress.
We use knowledge to hold ourselves above all others,
expatriate patriots.
We are the land of minority rule.
We are the land of lay-offs and bail-outs.
We huddle our masses into our cities to beg for change.

We have no conscience.

We are making history as we speak.
Start your engines.
Shake hands.
Two nations, under god.
Hallelujah,
play ball.

**

Sweat more in peace, bleed less in war.
Diplomacy works. Except in this case.
It seems that breath no longer means what it used to.
Does anyone hear the planes before they are shadows on the streets?
We choose what we want to pass-on to our children. Except in blood.
Even in blood though,
we are learning to engineer choice, to manufacture choice, to disregard choice.

The boys look just like their dad.
This is their mother's burden.
War is their mother's burden—
the sound of one soldier dying.

**

A round fired from an M-16A1 travels at a speed at least as fast as time.
What power to be handed death—
to be given the future.

This does strange things to the mind.
Each moment feels like getting away with something.
A soldier is not trained in diplomacy,
instead given the tools to enforce—
when you go, most of you are going to die.
A soldier is proof of diplomacy's end.
A round fired from an M-16A1 travels at least as fast as words.

**

Now we have experienced the horror, the loss, the pain, the contempt, the confusion—

now we have experienced the fallibility of being the strongest.
The world is too big to patrol, too small to keep others at arms-length.

Now we have experienced the reality of bombs, tanks and fighter planes in plain sight, machine guns along the morning commute, concrete barricades, evacuation plans, snipers, conspiracy's reach and hatred as common as motherhood and apple pie.

We are making history as we speak.
O truth you will always change.
O America, of course.

THE SLOW WAKING OF THE MIND

EVER SO QUIETLY

You could have it and not know it—
not know until something opens the door,
sets it off,
wakes it up,
shines the light of day and that dark fucker.

You could know it and still do little about it.
I know a woman who graduated high school
and didn't go to college because her dad didn't
think she would do any good.
Her name is Barb.
She stagnated in her father's home.
He abused her and her mom.
She started having epileptic seizures.
They got worse and worse and worse.
She's now medicated to the point of drooling
in a group home, a prisoner of her own mind.
Her mom died of cancer.
Her dad is an old, old man.
I used to visit her twice a week.

The addict mind begins to creep in
at the first sign of weakness,
carving slowly into itself until
the bottom drops out.
I know where mine comes from—
Irish and Scottish blood,
Canadian and Native American blood,
Mom's blood and dad's blood,
ghosts of ghosts of ghosts.
I know when mine started—
as a child chasing the blind high
of sugar which brought me near orgasm,
then finding a Penthouse as a teenager

which added another blind high pursuit;
the summer I was 17 and lost my virginity
to a girl who was much younger and had big tits
and said *I'm bored, you wanna do it with me?;*
when I drank whiskey for the first time
with Chad Rizzuto before a school dance,
hiding with a bottle behind the carriage house
of the Granger Homestead;
when I got high and drunk with friends
before making our way across town
for a senior class picnic;
when I went to basic training and gained self-confidence;
when I came home with my new confidence
and became the big fish in the little pond;
when I then left home to be the big fish in a bigger pond.

Excuses, excuses.
This shit was minor,
but the door was opening
to the rest of my life.
The bottom was dropping out
and I loved it
and I hated myself
and I loved it
and so it went.

I don't know what has happened to Barb
since I left.
It's been years now.
I miss her.
Maybe I'll visit when I'm home next.

LADY

She says my body is her sustenance,
I am the candle flame tracing her hungry silhouette,
heavy blooded sax and incessant snare drum,
my eyes are closed, her touch is velvet.

Heavy blooded sax and incessant snare drum,
I'm having a hard time breathing her bluenote voice.
She says my body is her sustenance,
I'm swinging from her hips in the dim light.

Night has coughed up streetlights and jazz,
my eyes are closed, her touch is velvet.
Following directions on a matchbook and my palm,
I am the candle flame tracing her hungry silhouette.

Following directions on a matchbook in my palm,
I'm swinging from her hips in the dim light.
Night has coughed up streetlights and jazz.
I'm having a hard time breathing her bluenote voice.

AN EVERYDAY FRIDAY NIGHT

After you say goodnight, I can't look myself in the face.

I am becoming something much larger than myself,
and you lie, greedy and naked in my eyes.

My spine retches, the room's on fire
with my hot breath and chattering nerves.

I am becoming something much larger than myself,
and you lie greedy and naked in my eyes.

Leaves will die and freeze under
the weight of January midnights
before I will find a proper hole
to bury myself in.

I am becoming something much larger than myself,
and you lie, greedy and naked in my eyes.

After your goodnight, I forced myself to look in the mirror
expecting the answer to be carved in bold across my forehead.

I am becoming something much larger than myself,
and you lie, greedy and naked in my eyes.

STILL, MADMAN

I know how to speak
to the living and the dead.
A lost language
that falls from my lips
like the second nature of a child
reaching for a flame.
Dangerous conversations

exposing the nature of hopelessness.
A need to feel something,
like hands in the belly
of a body in a hospital morgue
exposing inertia's last call.
It's a wonder we exist at all.

The living should be able to handle themselves.
The dead look nothing like I was taught.

HANDS I

Lazy day today in the sun through the
windshield. Lazy with the window rolled down,
with last night still playing through nerves,
with an occasional beat accompaniment to a song
barely above static in a long stretch
between Little Rock and Austin.

Lazy. Leaving her softly behind. Leaving
for the gold rush of change, pins and
needles of the unknown, licking their chops
over possibility. The animals.
They just do as they're told.
The truck barrels on.

WELCOME TO TEXAS

Juxtaposed with an unlikely six-hour jazz session
on a straining, static and likely below-the-radar
bible-belt AM station, the featureless August midnight
blacktop and black backdrop beyond the headlights
on route 30 outside of Jonesborough
is a lonely straight-through stretch
from Little Rock to the Texas border. Just
southwest of Hope, the jazz stuck
in some recess. Quiet, incessant, soft
saxbasspianocornettrumpetsnare
lowing their mellow rap in my mind's corner.
Playing to an empty club
save for the one man in the suit and loose tie,
eyes closed and harmonizing
with his thin rocks glass, and the sad woman
in the midnight-blue strapless.
Slow turn and sway and swish. Heels
on the empty dance floor. The road kept on.
Sunrise caught me somewhere
between Hope and the border
and I read the sign in its lone star largess, jazz
and dawn aching through.
The crazy riff of sage
and red-eyed 80 miles per hour.

CORPUS CHRISTI

I wake to the wilderness in her eyes and a futile wish for cool air from the ceiling fan. Morning coffee and a cigarette on the porch. Shafts of sun and smoke tendrils. The coffee still too hot to sip. Unhurried, our talk is hushed and spare.

She mourns the death of the local dive bar. Its small-town heyday of loud townies anchored till 2 am, drunk fists pounding on the bar. 3rd shift patrons with 8 am bottles of Bud. It's the simple loss that hurts the most.

Sundress and bare feet in the passenger seat. Her hair dancing. She plays with the wind out her window. Rearview mirror a greening season in bright retreat. Nothing but wide-open. Tires humming their miles-song.

Her echo won't let me let go. I wake alone under the stars with home a thousand miles away. Shoulders of gravel and ground tires. Wilderness. I'm told Corpus Christi means the body of Christ. Maybe there I'll say the hardest things I have to say.

A LOVE ONCE

Twenty minutes of side-strokes, back floats and the crawl
keep her pregnant body fit.
She is fluid in water—
free motion and weightlessness.
Her feet flutter, arms extended to pull sleekly both bodies—
two worlds suspended—
toward the shore.

THE DISTINCTION OF DUSK

As the sky fades I light my pipe
and settle into the belly of the canoe.

Geese are arriving. One pair at a time,
sometimes two. Their song in flight echoes

as they pass on the far side of the island nearby.
It is different than the song that signals their circling.

Different still than their song when they finally descend.
Into the water they careen feet-first.

Wings wide as Spring.
Breasting water and pollen film.

A cacophony of clucks and growls and sharp honks,
haggling with geese that have already settled on the water.

To float close enough is to hear their pinion feathers
rattle like playing cards in bicycle spokes,

and with ample light, see muscles working
at their shoulders and breast.

To see the outstretched tongue
of the loud lead bird as he wails.

To see each white belly feather as they arc by.
To see water splatter ahead of their webbed feet

across the still surface.
After a time they float, still and silent as decoys,

as the few remaining pairs arrive. Some land directly on the island.
Others sing and circle and sing and splash down.

8:45 and like clockwork they have all made their way
to nests in the shadow that is the island.

One last blaze of voices and, assured that all are accounted for,
they go silent or murmur beneath my hearing.

ALEIDA

My wife's water broke in the passenger seat of our Jetta in the hospital parking garage.
We laughed at our luck till we cried,
just as much out of being scared.
First-born daughter in my arms 22 November hours later,
I said her name a dozen times,
smelled her swaddled newness,
promised her that my devils would not be hers.

THE CONSEQUENCE OF RAIN

It has traveled from Kansas, having rolled down off the Rockies to spend a long weekend falling on early fields of alfalfa and on spring-green Mt. Sunflower, Cathedral of the Plains and Potawatomi Indian Reservation. It soaked Tallgrass Prairie as it swaggered up to the Ozarks. Passed De Soto and Cape Girardeau, Lake Egypt and the Ohio River, followed the Western Kentucky Parkway past Bardstown, drove through Daniel Boone National Forest gaining speed up the western slope of Cumberland Mountain to Wharncliff, over the Alleghenies and the Appalachians, over the North Fork of the Shenandoah and Skyline Drive at Harrisonburg where it slowed at Dickey Ridge, rolled into Falls Church and stalled.

Three days rain is falling and our grass and trees, our soil, our skin and cars and streets, our patios and boats and children's toys, our geese and dogs and strollers, our Senators and housing developments and homeless and fracking pads and coal scars and catchment ponds, our windows and lawn chairs, our yard tools, our newspapers and rivers and garbage cans and storm drains, our fish and crayfish and racoons and deer, our farm fields and cattle and chickens, our wetlands and public lands and private lands, our stop signs and school buses, our grocery carts and lakes and utility poles, our flowerbeds and swing-sets, our angels and demons are all tasting.

Three days rain is in love with everything.
Calls and feeds and exiles all things the same.
This land. This flooded mind.

MAKE BELIEVE

There is always a tension, however slight.
It isn't a need to drink at day's end or even a one-track rush to the bed of a woman.
It isn't a desire for attention or an uncontrollable anger lying in wait like a bayou gator.
It's a quiet intensity.
Enough to make you believe you are a good person.
Enough to heal for now.
Enough to gut-hook you into forgetting.
Enough to give you a new excuse.

HANDS II

Again the picture shifts.
My hand is visible—
aching joints, battered knuckles,
scarred gold band
against the angle of guitar strings.

Here the picture becomes
the newborn's perspective—
an angle of light
through a morning window—
the slow waking of the mind.

HOW EASY THE SPIRAL

What else is there besides fish and mayflies,
water and rocks, sky and woods?
What else besides bills and telemarketers, car repairs and groceries?
What is there besides greening bushes and returning geese?
Finches at the feeder and cardinals in the distance?
What else besides Wednesday garbage day, infidelity, diapers, dishes,
whiskey and picking up dog shit in the yard?
What else is there besides open windows in the afternoon and Grateful
Dead or Metallica on the breeze?
What else besides prescription drugs?
Temporary salvation and going through the motions?
Today is tomorrow's deep breath.
There is no changing course.

BECAUSE YOU WANTED TO KNOW

I haven't taken my Prozac in two days.
Expect anger.
Expect me to grit my teeth.
Expect frustration.
Expect me not to listen.
Expect me to be lazy
Expect me to get fired up about every half-cocked idea
Expect me to be intolerant.
Expect me to lose control of my libido.
Expect me to have a hard time getting through breakfast without thinking about sex or porn sites or 900 numbers or old girlfriends.
Expect me to want to drink.
Expect nothing good to come from that.
Expect me to yell at the dog for not keeping her nose out of my face
Expect me to be able to do anything.
Expect me to be funny.
Expect me *to you fucking idiot* everyone who doesn't drive right.
Expect me to want to run all night.
Expect me to have unlimited energy.
Expect me to defy all expectations.
Expect me to feel worthless.
Expect me to jerk-off in the shower.
Expect me to surround myself with people who make me feel good.
Expect me to expect that from any given woman.
Expect me to want to run.
Expect me to work myself to death.
Expect me to get into trouble.
Expect me to ignore the truth.
Expect me to be very persuasive.
Expect me not to be hungry.
Expect that I'll have a headache.
Expect me to drive too fast.
Expect me to drive drunk.
Expect that I'll be lost.
Expect that I'll be the center of attention.
Expect that I won't know how to talk to you.
Expect that I'll try and it'll come out all wrong.
Expect that my logic will make sense only to me.
Expect that this may never end.

ON EXISTING

It has nothing to do with the girl.
She just happened to be walking
by when spring arrived—
her presence was incidental.

But it did arrive—
a quiet exclamation of new
Maple buds and chickadee song and
grass still too wet to mow but too long
to let go another week.

I walk with my hands in my pockets.
I'm not sure what to make of this—
new buds, birdsong, grass, the girl—
I have done nothing, and spring is here.

HARD WINTER

The river is up.
The lake is up.
It's been a hard winter, but now there's water enough to stave off drought. Water enough that a few trout may last longer in the larger, cooler pools. Enough that bass will get the fattest they've been in the lean past decade.

But what is lean and what is abundant?
Fish are found drying on the shore,
birds and fox and raccoon are fed well;
the flora wilts further from drying banks,
a muskrat finds once submerged branches for its den;
the lake is frozen solid, the first time in 20 years,
a fox and her kits find an easy path from the island
to search out dinner;
runoff has flooded both lake and stream—
water, plastic bags, rotting leaves, tennis balls, sticks and branches clog
every eddy, cove and slack stretch of water;
several smallmouth are carried over the dam
and so starts a new population in the river below.

It has been a hard winter.
Spring has the color of more than enough.

CARRY ME, RIVER

The Mississippi long before I could see it.
The Mississippi from Front Street in Memphis. Twain's
watery highway.
Sawyer's freedom.
Hemingway's solid shifting lake.
Everything's been said and I don't want to talk anyhow.

The Mississippi from Front Street.
The Mississippi from Coahom County
The Mississippi at Rosedale.
The Mississippi by dugout canoe.
The Mississippi at Island 69.
The Mississippi with coffee over a campfire.
The Mississippi with John Rusky.
The Mississippi with a guitar and a bottleneck.
The Mississippi at the bottom of a whiskey bottle.
The Mississippi behind levees.
The Mississippi next to a hunting camp
and a bobcat hanging empty by its hind legs.
O Mississippi, everything's been said.
O Mississippi, you big-bodied brown woman.
O Mississippi, you sly musician.
O Mississippi, you slave owner, you freedom fighter.
O Mississippi, you street fighter.
O Mississippi, you keeper of the dead.
O Mississippi, you rail-bed to hell, you righteous current.
O Mississippi, you steady rider.
O Mississippi, you gambler.
O Mississippi, you paddle wheel.

O Mississippi, it's me.
O Mississippi, you could care less.

GOD BLESS THE BLUES

thank fucking god for that guitar
making the most of his chance in
hell whiskey with two ice cubes
playing amphetamine blues harp
till he draws blood, howling
I can't hear fast enough
or moan low enough
another two fingers and two ice cubes
I catch her coal-glow look
there was no way I could've given
first and no way I couldn't return
lyrics that narrate the rest of my night
come in my kitchen, she'll purr
one more time I nod
whiskey with two ice cubes
because rocks is pretentious
and neat is a shot
let's be honest

THAT IMMENSE BREATH

Yesterday on the river,
the old man spoke in roiling current
and half-buried bleach-white branches.
Heading upstream, hugging the shoreline
to avoid thousand-yard barges and the Coast Guard
tug snagging stranded buoys,
we paddled past lifetimes of conversation
gouged from the rip-rapped banks, past forty,
fifty-foot trees beached thirty-foot above water-line
like broken toothpicks discarded after a dinner
of catfish, fried okra, black-eyed peas and sweet tea.

When you're on the Mississippi you're on river time.
I kept waiting for something to happen.

We made a fire among driftwood on a sandbar
and boiled water for coffee while the river slipped past
silent as the smoke from the black walnut we were burning.
I crossed the tracks of beaver that had gnawed down brush
and dragged them to the water, a raccoon's small hand prints
following the waterline for dead fish, the ghost of coyotes
wrestling around higher up the bank—
tails swishing sand, paws, bellies, backs and snouts imprinted.
The river is down 18-foot from normal
for this time of year and we're all taking advantage.

When spring sends its runoff
from the Continental Divide and Ohio River valley,
from Canada and the northern plains,
our tracks here will be washed away—
disappearing in that one immense breath.

PUT DOWN YOUR LOAD

What was I looking for in those Delta waters?
What made me speak to the fat, slow Sunflower?
Whose reflection was I looking for?
I stood down her kudzu'd bank that once anchored
the near side of a bridge that led to miles of
cotton fields while Dockery's ghosts wandered
the grounds like a languid July breeze.
The water was deep from the edge,
mud slick and quietly hungry looking.
I had no pole to fish with. No line. No bait.
So I played harmonica for the Sunflower.
I played for all of its ghosts.
I played for old catfish and carp and bass.
I played for the long shadows of the cotton gin and its long barn.
I played for the blues that were born there
and the blues that died there.
I played for Keith Dockery McLean and Joe Rice and Will.
I played for the 100 casino billboards on Route 61.
I played for Po' Monkeys juke in his gold Cadillac
and tractor out back.
I played for the only woman in the gentlemen's club just south of
Memphis at Wednesday lunchtime.
I played for empty Clarksdale storefronts.
I played for Frank L Ratliff and the Riverside Hotel
and the room where Bessie Smith died.
I played for the crossroads and its gas station and Popeye's Chicken.
I played for Sonnyboy's gravestone
and the pocket-whiskey folks had left.
I played for Mound Bayou.
I played for the ace of spades I found on a street in Ruleville.
I played for Joe's Tamale Place.
I played for Farrish Street and Cleophis Dennis' Shoe Shop.
I played for split level sidewalks in Tunica.
I played for Parchman Farm
and the trustees on the long row and for the gas chamber.
I played for shotgun shacks and Charlie Patton's daughter, Rose.
I played for Robert Johnson's and Tommy Johnson's souls.
I gave my breath because I had nothing left to give.
I played for the Sunflower and then left empty for home.

HANDS III

Scar tissue as memory—
a road map print across knuckles—
abbreviated Atlas, extended forecast.
Here I see Nuremberg and there a fallow cotton field.
Tread crossed swirls,
Euphrates in green—
tendons swim through the engravings
which always start white
then turn red—
braids of carbon, destruction and repair.

CAM

Our son was pulled from the river of his mother in mid-August.
He will grow with the sound of cicadas
and Crosby, Stills, Nash and Young in his ears—
will join this landscape with the final late day warmth
of summer in his backbone
and the half-sunrise chill of autumn in his steps.
Our son has joined his sister and all I wish can be only that.

THE MUSIC FROM THE NOISE

Music of water signing under a spinning sky. Birds and branches; clouds and stony sandbars; rotten trees half submerged and sun barely below the hardwood treeline; beaver crashing a pool; thrusting bedrock; eddies and slight bubble-foam; trees hanging spring leaves and emerging caddis; trout and bass and sunfish and sucker.

Close to the city you sing, O water, under a spinning sky, under a slight exhaust breeze, under burnt-out campfires and rusting cans of Budweiser and plastic bags and broken glass, under persistent helicopter chop and sirens and traffic and construction, under busted sewer overflow, under inner-tubes and tires and life-jackets and rope and bags of trash and tennis balls.

Close to my heart you sing, O water, to the flow of my blood, to the bends at my joints, the riot of my thoughts.

WHAT IT BOILS DOWN TO

There is a street and three-car-an-hour traffic,
which is louder if I pay attention.
But if I don't,
the volume turns down
to the crickets in the grass
a whisper of those head-to-tail-lights
and the tumble-clink of ice
in the glass that left a sweat ring
on the porch board after I picked it
up and took a sip of dilute whiskey.

BY THE RIVER

Hundreds of minnows have congregated
in chest-deep water,
churning themselves into a knot.
A galaxy of twisting flesh in cloudy water
like it could be lifted
dripping and alive
by your late-summer grasp—
a body of slick, silver-grey.

I imagine you back-lit
by the soft sounds of the river,
a sigh in wet white,
holding up that galaxy,
water lapping at your waist.

In an instant the tangle flexes,
untangles,
and is gone.

JONAH

I can't begin to understand
the sacrifice of childbirth.
He was her third cesarean, this little man.
Out of her belly and into the world,
following his sister and brother.
In recovery, we wondered at his perfect features
while we agreed on a name
and I knew in my guts
he would be her last.

JULY NIGHTSONG

Once the early rains have passed
the cicadas taunt the breeze.
They relent only to nightfall—
weakening fits of clicks and rattles—
until, content that the long-drawn day
has wilted, they leave the crickets
to serenade the cooling sky.

This old song declares itself,
calls from the wisteria and bamboo,
the oscillation of brittle sound
caught in the ink and paper
of a life not yet discovered,
yet still rising,
rising above even this.

A FRONT PUSHES IN

The last of the daylight sneaking off, raindrops
from the pines fall heavy on the cabin's tin roof
while the kids, wrapped in blankets, listen to a story.

My place is here on the dock,
facing a northwest wind that carries the rain,
a steady mist that grays each direction.

Across the river the lights of the restaurant are
still lit. Locals on barstools facing beers,
a blonde bartender in a generous tank top and last call.

The pine shoreline leans with the storm. A jagged boundary.
Chorus of black above the almost-black of the water.
The age-old arc of this story will continue long after I'm gone.

Yesterday the kids soared as bobbers sprung to life, interrupting
a perfectly still surface. Shockwaves from a dozen catfish, one by one
filling their maw with a fat worm, then filling childhood's memory.

Cast after cast from the dock, my fly cruising the calm world beneath
the windblown world above. Tonight I imagine
the raw poetry of a Northern pike annihilating the line
between the two. Miles off, the rolling growl of thunder.

THIS CURRENT'S COURSE

Nameless stream, a whisper among boulders and tree roots,
a tired whisper after the dam holding an acre-sized beaver pond
breached, let loose a river from up the mountain, straightening the
meandering curves of this small seam, bounding,
fanning wide into the moss, fern, rock and pines
before circling back and rushing on.

From the relative depths of a dark cut
beneath a knot of exposed birch roots,
an eager brook trout attacks my fly.
Bright gem catching a glint of sunlight in
this almost accidental universe.
Giant in its place here.

VIEW FROM THE FIRE TOWER

I'm reminded of a poem by Gary Snyder,
written while he was a fire lookout in the North Cascades.

Months at a time he'd spend in service and solitude.
Thinking.

From six stories up, I can see the attraction.
Sprawling topography of mountainsides and valleys, so much

softer from this height, stitched one to the other in shades of green,
patchwork blanket of pine and hardwoods. Hawks rising

higher and higher on thermals, still suspended far below. Candid
conversations with the wind. Graceful, shifting, gigantic

balance of dawn's hue and starry dusk.
Active meditation on a passive existence. This tower,

like his, the center of its own universe, one
of billions of centers each revolving around each.

Tribes gathering in celebration.
A choir looking skyward for its voice.

LEAVING AFTER DARK

There's a moment when
the sound of my footsteps on gravel,
and the creak of my pack,
and the hugeness of breath in the fields
and night in its soaking weight
all go away—

when, like color leaving a face, moonlight drains
from the road, the thin grass, the low yawning hills—

when the owl
swoops in giant flight
to snatch a mouse and I feel and hear
the roiling air,
the thump of their meeting—

when I am,
and with eyes closed,
begin to hum something quiet to myself.

WEST TO WATER

By mid-Chicago to LA it still hasn't hit me. Sprawling canyon salt flat scrub brown and mountains crawl below. I carried on three fly rods and a book of Jim Harrison's poetry. Our platinum blond, plump-lipped stewardess calls me Skippy. She won't take cash for a beer.

Idaho. Three months ago, this trip was two friends, wishful thinking and barstools in Upstate New York. I had just left my job to follow a dream of independence. Grant was trying to get his head around independence after losing his job. By our third round it was unanimous.

Here, I am slow motion. Layers of break-neck life peeling away. I know it's the wide-open expanse of frontier plainsong. Forever rolling and howling as the speedometer pushes 85 and The Grateful Dead wander their highway through Althea in Nassau. I am small here.

Gas station coffee, grain elevators, rail cars, Friday night lights, onions, grapes, magpies, llamas, cottonwood groves, sunflowers, sage, corn, wheat, cattle, chukar, grouse, desert quail, winding roads, canyon, famous potatoes. One lone strip club hiding over the county line.

Hot copper-white and sage canyon floor. We sit in camp chairs with beers, grilling meat for lunch in the weak shade of a nearby tree. Driftwood and brush flood-woven 8 feet up in its branches. On the other side of the willows the desert river pretends to mind its own business.

4 a.m. Roadside sage and gravel shoulder chase the curving road, a cold ghost-gray in our headlights. We make the Sawtooth Basin by sunup. Eggs, sausage, homemade white toast and coffee in Stanley. Outside, thin smoke from a small campfire, quiet talk, mountains. It's 27 degrees.

To get here, switchbacks had us coming and going. We park in a pull-off, pull on waders and step-skid-step to the water. This seventy-yard stretch runs twelve feet deep and gin clear right from the edge. Sun finds us at 10:38. Smoke from last season's fire a thin film in the air.

We spot a moose as we haul the jet boat down highway 26. Big black body in full stride a half-mile out into amber waves of grain. Her pine and brush foothills another quarter-mile off. A combine leads a yellow dust cloud across the next immense field. The sky looks like rain.

Mack truck river hauling the ass-end of mammoth runoff. There's no thinking at this pace. We drift, I sling. Wail full-on gun-shots into slack eddies, under thick brush, against cliff wall undercuts and grass-sand banks. Swings and short-strikes. Dusk drops on our run back to the launch.

I know he's going to take before he does. Everything's right. Cast, distance, depth, slower than river speed drift, *Folsom Prison Blues* playing in my head. The fly touches bottom a couple times, tumbles from the riffle into the pale green. I look him in the face, *good one* he says. *Good one.*

An hour and a half drive north. The sun burns off the morning haze and the Tetons get to their feet. Riverside parking and talk of big fish. forty-minutes downstream from the truck, we scramble from a game trail into the river. At thigh deep, I'm the knife at a gunfight. Even so, I'm in.

From where I stand, frontiersmen once contemplated their purpose in this landscape, the panorama of destiny. But right now, sports are still crowding the fly shop counter in town to rent an experience, leaving the big fish here with me to rise carelessly, thinking the coast is clear.

Here, life stripped down. Immense. Unapologetic. A hard-worked, callous hand. It doesn't take long. I'm losing myself. Finding my self.

Home is two hours ahead and a world away. Failing marriage, kids a fleeting thought and phone call at day's end. My mind quiet and full.

Mesa Falls, Ashton, Rexburg, Rigby fill our rearview mirror. Windows down, simmering late-afternoon sun, we're on the other end of the gauntlet and there's nothing pressing to say. The last eight days packed tight in my tired, calloused hands, ready to throw like a sneaky left in the final round.

These five rivers are forever in my blood. These days and miles and fish and landscapes are forever in my blood. Tomorrow is 9/11 and our flight back east. Tonight we drink bucket-beers at the stock car races. I feel like a good fight or some Howlin' Wolf but I'm hungry and still have to pack.

12:20 a.m. Wheels-down in Rochester. Shuttle ride to the car, Army duffel, pack and rods at my feet, two frowning wives cluck about Yellowstone's rustic amenities. One husband nods, Good fishing? I nod back. Montana? he asks. Idaho. My voice is ten-day gravel and far from being home.

SHOOTING DARTS IN ALASKA

When the day falls and the thin promise of neon rises, the brown liquor and beer go down easier and with more truth and there's a life-or-death feel to the whole thing. Everything flies true and I'm just as apt to walk to the docks—crowded sleeping silhouette-mass of mast wire, swing arms, buoys and hulls—and stare at the moon on the water and let my girl run wild in my mind, as I would be to jump into a barroom mêlée between two hopeless drunk men over a homely drunk woman, if only to feel the blunt sting of one lucky punch finding my cheek before dispatching the soup-bones on anybody close enough to catch them.

The gravity of our last night north of the 49th parallel was settling in. A week in-flight, afloat, on-foot and on the road in a small portion of the 17-million-acre Tongass National Forest now reaching its end. There was an other-worldly aspect to being there. Outside of the cruise ships careening to the sky from the main drag and local shoebox storefronts in the shadows plying their trade. Outside the chaos of the tourist-herds migrating from here to there and back in wide-brimmed hats and khaki shorts and sandals. Further outside. The rainforest mountains and calving glaciers in topaz brilliance. Further. An orca in the wide salt spotted from our pontoon plane. Further. Gauze-thick clouds swallowing snow-capped horizons and bear and wolf tracks on sand bars. Further, son. *Go further.*

Our days were spent surrounded by the old growth spruce and devil's club and ferns and fireweed, in rivers thick with fish, from the salt to our feet and on to its glacial headwaters. Pinks and chum and dollies, but pinks mostly. Humpies. Angry, bright, toothy, headlong-in-leopard-spot haymakers on almost every cast. Fish six-to-eight pounds and the occasional humped male pushing weight to double digits. So many you could feel the hit on your swung fly and bury a fair-hooked solid strip-set before they hit your swung fly. So many that you let even shitty casts drift. So many that we made things more challenging by throwing dry flies—pink gurglers the size of hummingbirds—just to watch them rise and blindly fumble around after the fly behind those un-earthly kyped beaks. We imagined them with a voice like Barney Gumble, while our own voices, hollering *Humpaaaayyy!!!* echoed up and down the river like kids with a new cuss word on the playground.

And now, a week spent and our last night just reaching good-and-loud, we're throwing darts with frontier aim, like there are bears at the door and we're warming up for the main event. The beer and brown liquor speaking truth and the seven of us, rough-hewn and comfortable with the uncomfortable. Explorers, seekers, hunters, letting go of as much as we had gathered. We were hand-scrawled maps on bar napkins and midnight advice between rounds while the juke-box rambled and burned.
Park here.
Fish anywhere from there on up.
Can't wait to see how many rods you bust.
You need a beer.

Prodigal sons making peace with tomorrow's journey home, shouldering a dart board confidence and capability that snipes trip-twenties or the walk-off double bull and roars fuck yea, bitches and shoves somebody. While the deck hands and locals go on spending paychecks, getting good and drunk and loud like there's no tomorrow, avoiding themselves and happy for our distraction.

THE FINE LINE BETWEEN FLIGHT & INERTIA

Standing in a river. Skirting a field of clover. Paddling a canoe. Walking to my car. Sitting in my tree stand. Watching my daughter's track meet. Raking leaves. Brushing my teeth. Running a trail in the pines. Taking the garbage out. Landing a fish. Leaning in for a kiss. Talking with my sons. Washing dishes. Picking up dog shit. Leaving a funeral. Sweating after sex on a blanket in the tall grass. Idling at a stop light. Pausing mid-mountain in the snow. Dressing my first deer of the season. Drinking coffee on the porch. Casting to rising fish. Warming my hands by the fire. Losing track of my limbs. Seeing no color in anything. Fighting to sleep. Sitting death-still on the couch. Staring at the same electrical outlet for hours. Letting full days pass unattended. Managing, somehow, to still get enough work done. Wanting to liquidate every last piece of my gear. Closing my eyes for a full three seconds at speed in traffic. Breathing with the bottom tenth of my lungs. Vacating any and all feeling except rage. Tasting copper in my throat. Clenching my jaw against *fuck it all.* Clinging to the sound of my kids in the house.

Yet somehow
a bird in flight, full-throated calling

into the universe of its view,
will stop me in my tracks.

Eyes skyward, searching
for the small flame in empty space.

No one can fly for the bird
or give it song. Both are an ability

possessed individually. Gained
through the ignorance of falling.

The innocence of mimicry.
The discovery of consequence.

Tangible proof of the fine line
between life and death.

Hypothesis turned fact
in the first pulse of air under the decisive weight

of the unknown.
A bird in flight is unbridled joy.

Its song a reminder
that those heights still exist.

ON THINKING ABOUT IRONIC PARALLELS

The dogs bolted again. Didn't even feign worry about consequence. Out the door and directly into the thicket behind the house before I had hung my keys and put my prescriptions on the counter.

Sunlight, fresh air, the world splitting wide open at their first burst off the top step of the porch. Brains suddenly saturated with dopamine that would carry them through hours of cattail swamp thorn brush deer trail freedom. Eating dead squirrel deer raccoon flesh, winter scavenger-worn vertebrae and carpal bones swallowed whole. Rolling in fox and coyote shit and anything with the glorious smell of rot. Eyes black on fire. Ears pinned back. Ravenous as addicts. There is no tomorrow.

I used to chase them. Rush to put on boots. Whistle-shout my way into the woods. Pissed off and cursing. Vowing to throttle them both. Mud spray up my pantlegs, thorns raising lines of blood, I'd keep at it till I found them. Cowering in a slow sulk to me with tails curled tight. I'd snap leashes on their muddied, stinking collars while they came down from their brains-full of junk. Nose to tail covered, tongues lolling, panting, chests full of kickdrum, bellies aching to betray.

They pay four days for their run. Rotten puke turning out bones. Liquid shit. Joints refusing to loosen. They limp to their water, lap slowly. Dog food goes untouched. Whine on their bed as the consequence of their blind instincts works through their intestines.

Now, after so many times, I don't chase. I'll drive streets in town to see if I can catch them in the open, but then return home and wait for a call from a stranger who found them on their porch, in their yard or nosing circles with their dog, their names and my number on their collars. I've resigned myself to the fact that the call might deliver me to them dead on the side of the road.

On the back steps in the March afternoon sun, waiting, I've lost the anger. My own destructive blind runs. I'm beginning to understand. I grab my keys one more time.

OVER MONTANA.
HIS FIRST MOUNTAINS.

Below us, the northern Rockies assert
their dominance over the landscape.
That's how he looks at them.

How he manages some sort of context
to reconcile the completely foreign
reality they present to him. Back home

the highest peak is 5,344 feet.
Mt. Marcy in the Adirondacks.
Our mountains wouldn't even be

foothills down there, he says.
This is only his second flight, ever. First
time west. First in the daytime where he can

see the country of my stories
crawl below, sometimes in long,
cloudless stretches that end

with the curvature of the earth
on the horizon. Stories of places, wild
and immense. Stories he's grown up with.

We are headed to Alaska.
The country will only get bigger.
His estimation is confidently matter-of-fact,

placing what he knows against
the reality he's witnessing.
An exclamation that he now possesses

some of the same truth and awe that I hold.
As Idaho's rugged tapestry now sprawls into view,
I can almost hear the tumblers

of the lock fall into place. See his mind
spring open. The light in his face says
it's real. All of it is real.

NAKNEK AUGUST

Floating slowly across the shallows,
the imprints of bear and moose
are preserved in the gravel-mud bottom.

Arteries between a brush-tangled island
and rolling green-gold tundra.
The jut of mountains on the horizon

one beyond the other
in distinct pastel layers.
It takes a half-mile of progress

in the boat to change their positions
below the blue sky.
When the engine stops and our wake

slips softly away, we notice
just how complete the quiet is.
How there is nothing at all.

Talking seems disrespectful.
Here, *'luqruuyak*. Pike and their teeth.
Elsewhere, *taryaqvak*, *qakiiyaq*, *sayak*,

talaariq, *amaqaayak*, *iqallugpik*, *culugpauk*.
Each an indigenous story returning
to home water. A month past the midnight sun,

the pure spread of stars is close
enough now to swirl your finger through
by eleven-thirty. Nights are beginning

their burdensome return. In my dream
I have come from the wilderness
to the wilderness. Here, awake at the river

before dawn, I breathe deeply
with new lungs. The only sound
is wolves howling.

ORIGIN'S NAME

this is big country
with a big sky
and great big shoulders

each boot print springs back
forgiving green-gold tundra
alders like herds

bear grass and sockeye
this river and her stones
are not waiting for me

not looking over her shoulder
as she leaves around the bend
there's a canyon upstream

if you can believe it
lasting artifact of ice
where she springs to run wild

belly full of char and grayling
wolves, moose and bear too
at least their tracks say so

fireweed and fall's beginning
as far as I can see
this is what was

if I follow
of course I will follow
so will my undoing

PRODIGAL SOCKEYE

We back across the river to give a big sow her space.
The fifty yards we offer is barely a few muscular bounds away.
She could care less about us, we know, until we impose.

43,000 of her kind gather in Katmai's bosom.
Sockeye scatter in cloud bursts from my feet.
Red and green divinity

by the thousands in cold current.
Prodigal sockeye home from exile. Each fish an exponent.
Loaves and fishes echo from childhood Sunday school.

A communion of body and blood.
Boundless pounds of flesh each day
from one congregation, tithed to another.

We bear silent witness. Sudden believers.
Winter will come and this return will somehow be enough.
As it was and ever shall be.

WHEN YOU HOLD AN ALASKAN SALMON

you are the closest you'll ever be to your wild soul
you are distilled to instinct's base pair
adrenaline floods the void

the bronchioles in your lungs wait on bated breath
bones and mountains and children stop aging
it imprints in the freestone of your arteries

the strata of belief finds its unchelated order
its alchemy transforms the withered to wholehearted
you collect on childhood's investment

your prayer is spoken into thin air
your thanks are the ground beneath you
you're never more vulnerable

you are singled-out
vernacular matters little
you are a foreign imposition

you are the alien
suddenly, privilege makes sense
subsistence equals respect

division relents
you see color for the first time
you meet humility

it swallows the folly of greed
it rewilds what's been stolen
you want for nothing

you're willing to listen
wounds, scab-taut, heal but scar
you have your answer

it is a beginning and an end
you remember stories you'd forgotten
self-sufficiency's lightning bolt interrupts doubt

abundance becomes important
it has already fed generations
nature gives you her full attention

the sky is wide and wider and wider still
songs of cultures crescendo in the river's ribcage
sandhill cranes roar from beyond the alders

brown bears count the hundreds of million pulses
promises are made and made good
its mind and yours trade wild abandon

you never return to who you were

WHAT I WOULD'VE MISSED

in my stand above the creek
hawks and heron slip by
in flight at eye-height
sun fills the swale
giving away its depth
touches its brown dry height
just so and I see
the gentle rake of antlers
drifting silently through
two woodpeckers several jays
and their long volleys
a bald eagle's silent patrol
hillsides of running watercolor
chickadees like pole-sitters
on stalks of goldenrod
two slinking coyotes
two old hunters
in orange hats and vests
one black lab named Pete
(I heard one hunter call him)
wearing a collar bell
two shotgun reports
two pheasant flushed to safer cover
noisy thump of a hawk
narrowly lose its grip
on a fortunate squirrel
leaves explode then settle
tree branches spun
with glints of spider web
billowing slightly in the breeze
a blue heron in the creek
casting no shadow
as she hunts minnows
blue jays bolting into trees
a quick flare then landing
to tattle-tale to each other
across a field woodpecker
unexpected guest knocking
high up the tree
I can feel his insistence
in my spine twenty feet below
even these hills change shape
if I look long enough
morning's light in its own way
always.

THE GORY DETAILS

A red light stopped the progress of a dozen or so of us headed west on routes 5 & 20. The light at this intersection is longer than most since it has to cycle through six separate traffic patterns. It was 2:15 in the afternoon and the sun pouring through the windshield had caught the scar on my thumb in, truly, beautiful light.

I studied the way that it started slightly wider and softer on its proximal end, swerved left only slightly and finished narrower and shining on the distal end. Intersected at thee points where stitches left their coordinates, point-line-point, they looked like three paddles across a canoe in flat, open water.

I was fabricating a fly rod holder for my kayak. A couple short lengths of PVC pipe, jig saw, 18-volt cordless Dewalt with 3-eighths bit and a c-clamp to secure to the work-table. My daughter toddling on the patio, puddle to drying puddle from last night's storm.

I leveled the drill and pulled the trigger. Before my reaction-time could catch up with the situation, a bur grabbed the bit which grabbed the pipe which grabbed my thumb, halting the PVC and freeing the bit from the bur to instantly chew through the waist of my thumb and pin it against the pipe's opposite side.

There's more, of course. A litany of gory details. But sometimes it's not about the gory details. Sometimes it's about a red light, a scar and beautiful sunlight.

How many times in the last twenty years have I been caught in a long stare at this scar not looking at the scar at all? A thousand-yard plea through glazed-blank eyes. Depression's callous inertia.
How many times has a car horn cleared the fog eight, ten seconds after the light has turned green?

None of that matters. Right now, I remember letting a glistening bass disappear back to its darkness. My daughter squealing with joy in my lap as we paddle a little further to another patch of lily pads. This light is longer than most and I'm thankful for the time.

FOR DECADES I'VE HIDDEN

For decades I've hidden in the freedom of woods and water. Childhood nature now grown. Immersed, enjambed, one hushed exhale into the next in its circuital pentameter. Seasonal stanzas marking decades of attempted escape. There is no distance far enough.

The responsibility of life is far easier when left at the door on my way out. Cross the threshold empty handed, empty hearted and conspiring like thieves with my dark passenger. Arms around shoulders, nodding one-track affirmations into the green.

Ten thousand escapes. It takes ten thousand and one before I turn around and witness forty-eight years of junk mind wither then burn to its rhizomes. Wildfire clean. The past holds hazy in the air above the lake in its clear-eyed glacial depth. Nostalgia does not relent.

It's no longer enough to walk away. Cicadas' rattling syllables join the breeze coming down the glen. North, up and over heights of shale and hardwoods, the great snake lies dead as the Native story goes, after being killed by a young warrior, puking the heads of its dead as stones into the lake.

Eagles in flight name the southwest wind. Carry their purpose in wide gliding patrols. Nature witnessing itself. Sustaining order as I relearn the chemistry, biology and poetry of my own nature. A man revised. Enjambed again in the hushed celebration of presence.

DEAD RECKONING COLLECTIVE is a veteran owned and operated publishing company. Our mission encourages literacy as a component of a positive lifestyle. Although DRC only publishes the written work of military veterans, the intention of closing the divide between civilians and veterans is held in the highest regard. By sharing these stories it is our hope that we can help to clarify how veterans should be viewed by the public and how veterans should view themselves.

Visit us at:

deadreckoningco.com

@deadreckoningcollective

@deadreckoningco

@DRCpublishing

Follow MATT SMYTHE

mattsmythe.com

MATT SMYTHE hails from the Finger Lakes region of western New York. An Army veteran and lifelong outdoorsman, Matt suffers from an inability to sit still or follow well-worn paths. If he's not in the woods, or on the water, he's scheming ways to get there. His work has appeared in *Gray's Sporting Journal*, *The FlyFish Journal*, *The Drake*, *Southern Culture on the Fly*, *Revive*, *Midcurrent*, *TROUT Magazine*, *Blueline*, and other magazines and literary journals.

CPSIA information can be obtained
at www.ICGtesting.com
Printed in the USA
BVHW041357240522
637796BV00024B/178